Winnie the Pooh

Who Said, "Whoo"?

Eeyore loved warm, lazy days.
"Think I'll just sit here for a while and
take things nice and slow," he said to
himself. "There's nothing better than
doing nothing."

Suddenly, a loud noise came out of nowhere.

"WHOOO," it said.

"Who? It's just me, Eeyore," Eeyore answered back. "Who are you?"

"WHOOO," said the noise again. "WHOOOOOOO."

"I'm not going to be able to get any rest around here," said Eeyore. So he went off to find his friends to see if they could help him figure out who said, "WHO."

Eeyore found Pooh thinking very hard in his Thinking Spot. He told Pooh about the "WHO."

"You've come to the perfect place," said Pooh. "Now all I've got to do is think, think, think."

So Pooh thought...and thought...and thought.

"'WHO' you say?" asked Pooh.

"No," replied Eeyore. "*I* didn't say it. Someone else did. That's what I want to find out. Who said, 'WHO?' And what does it mean?"

"Well," said Pooh, listening really hard. "Whoever said, 'WHO' is not in my Thinking Spot. We'll have to go listen someplace else."

Soon, the two friends ran into Piglet.
"What are you looking for?" Piglet asked.
"We're on the hunt for a WHO," replied Pooh.
"Have you seen or heard one today?"

"No," replied Piglet. "I don't believe I have."

"Shh!" said Eeyore. "I think I hear something." He listened hard. "It sounds like a CHIRP."

"Birds chirp," said Piglet. "And I see a pair in that tree chirping to each other."

"What do you suppose they're saying?" asked Eeyore.

Piglet was certain he knew.

"One bird says, 'I think this tall tree is perfect for our nest,' and the other says, 'Oh, dear! I'm afraid of heights!'"

"Perhaps Rabbit heard the 'WHO,'" Piglet suggested. "You may want to ask him."

Pooh, Piglet, and Eeyore found Rabbit standing in front of his kitchen cupboard.

"Rabbit, have you heard a 'WHO?'" asked Eeyore.

But Rabbit wasn't paying attention. He had his own problem to solve.

"This must be the squeak I'm hearing," he said, opening the door of his cupboard. "'SQUEAK, SQUEAK, SQUEAK' all day long!"

Eeyore followed his ears once again.

"Better have a look over here, Rabbit," he said.

A family of mice was living in the bottom of Rabbit's vegetable bin, snacking on the corn he had just picked.

"SQUEAK, SQUEAK, SQUEAK," they said.

Eeyore tried very hard to understand what all the squeaking was about, but he just couldn't make any sense of it.

"What do you suppose they're saying?" he asked.

How Do Animals Communicate?

You know that an owl can't send e-mails to another owl, and a squirrel can't phone his cousin collecting acorns in a nearby tree. But animals do communicate with each other; through noises (such as squeaking, grunting, chirping or chattering), body language, (such as wagging tails, flapping wings, making funny faces) as well as through touch and scent.

This language might not make much sense to us, but to another animal, the message is crystal clear. And that's a good thing, because sometimes that message is really important. It could be a warning that danger is near or used for attracting other animals of the same species or kind.

Preschoolers learn by mimicking and playing games. This guessing game encourages your child to use his/her imagination, observing and listening skills, and reasoning abilities. Here's a game to play.

Step 1: On slips of paper, write down several names of different animals that make specific sounds (such as: lion, monkey, bird, owl, sheep, pig, duck, dog, cat, etc.) or paste pictures of various animals onto cards.

Step 2: Place the slips of paper or cards in a shoebox and shake them up. Then take turns with your child, reaching in and selecting one without looking.

Step 3: Ask your child to think of what sound the animal makes to talk to his friends. Then have him/her demonstrate the sound to you.

Step 4: Then it's your turn. Ask your child to say what animal you're mimicking.

"Well, now we know who said 'WHO,'" replied Eeyore. "It was Owl. And now I know what Owl's 'WHO' was trying to tell me. It was loud and clear."

"What's that?" asked Piglet.

"'WHO' in Owl talk means, 'sweet dreams,'" said Eeyore.

Everyone—even Owl himself—agreed.

And before they left for home, Pooh and his friends listened once more to the sounds of the animals talking. The Hundred-Acre Wood was filled with CHIRPING and CHATTERING and BUZZING and RIBBITING and SQUEAKING.

Earlier it seemed like a lot of noise, but now that he understood that animals talk to each other, it was all music to Eeyore's ears.

"Did you hear the 'WHO' again?" asked Owl. "Do you know who said it?"

"Yes!" said Eeyore. "It was you who said, 'WHO,' Owl—when you were snoring!"

"Oh, well, yes," said a slightly embarrassed Owl. "Owls do say 'WHO.' I, of course, knew that all along...."

The rustling leaves woke Owl with a start. "What happened?" he asked.

"Nothing," said Pooh. "You were taking a little nap."

There, on a branch, was Owl snoring. And when he opened his mouth wide, he made a deep, loud "WHO" sound.

"WHO," came a noise out of the blue. "WHO, WHO, WHO, WHO, WHOOOOOO!"

"That's the sound!" cried Eeyore. He followed the noise to a large tree and looked up. He could hardly believe his eyes.

"See this bee whirling around as she buzzes?" asked Owl. "She's leading the other bees over to these flowers she's found."

"Perhaps, I should follow the bee as well," said Pooh. "Bees always lead me right to honey."

"Yes," said Owl, yawning. "That sounds like an excellent idea. I'll just wait for you right here and take a little rest."

"Then you should come with us," said Eeyore. "Maybe you can help us find out who said, 'WHO' and what it means."

"If you look as well as listen, you'll be able to figure out what the animals are saying—even if you don't speak their language," Owl added. "Simply watch for clues."

"Those different sounds you heard are the animals talking to one another," said Owl.

"If they're talking, then why can't I understand them?" asked Eeyore.

"Because only a squirrel can understand another squirrel, and only a frog can understand another frog," Owl explained. "I, however, speak many different animal languages...."

So Pooh, Piglet, Rabbit, Eeyore, and Tigger all went to Owl's house to ask his advice.

Owl was about to take a nap, when his friends arrived.

"Hello, Owl," said Eeyore. "We've heard a lot of animals all making different sounds, but no one seems to know who said, 'WHO!'"

"I hear something over here," said Piglet, waving to Eeyore.

"CHATTER, CHATTER, CHATTER," said a trio of squirrels running up and down the trunk of a tree.

"I can't tell what they're chattering about," said Piglet.

"They suggest we seek some expert advice on this whole 'WHO' matter," guessed Pooh. "Owl will be able to help us for sure. After all, he knows practically everything about everything."

"Well, I did hear some loud, deep noises comin' from the pond," offered Tigger. "Let's go see, Donkey Boy."

At the pond, Eeyore poked his nose into the water and was greeted with a big, wet RIBBIT. Then another.

"Those two frogs are croaking, 'Howdy do at you, Eeyore!'" said Tigger.

Outside Rabbit's house, Tigger was bouncing by.

"Hoo-hoo-hoo! What's new?" he asked.

"Tigger always says, 'Hoo-hoo-hoo.' Maybe he's the one who said 'WHO,'" suggested Piglet.

"No," said Eeyore. "It was a loud, deep 'WHOOOOO.' It wasn't Tigger."

"Oh, I understand it!" said a flustered Rabbit, scowling at the mice.
"They're saying, 'My, Rabbit's corn is very tasty. We're going to help
ourselves to seconds and thirds and leave him none for his supper!'"